a gift for

....

from

....

with love

MANY MOONS
&
MOTELS

Many Moons
&
MOTELS

MANY MOONS
&
MOTELS

Poems of Love, Sorrow, & the Wild Woman

BY

Lexis Zenobia

A BOOK

MEANT

TO BE

CARRIED

WITH

YOU

When a page is found blank within this book,
write, draw, paint...
I encourage you to give it purpose,
like the towering tree it once was.

fire

air

water

earth

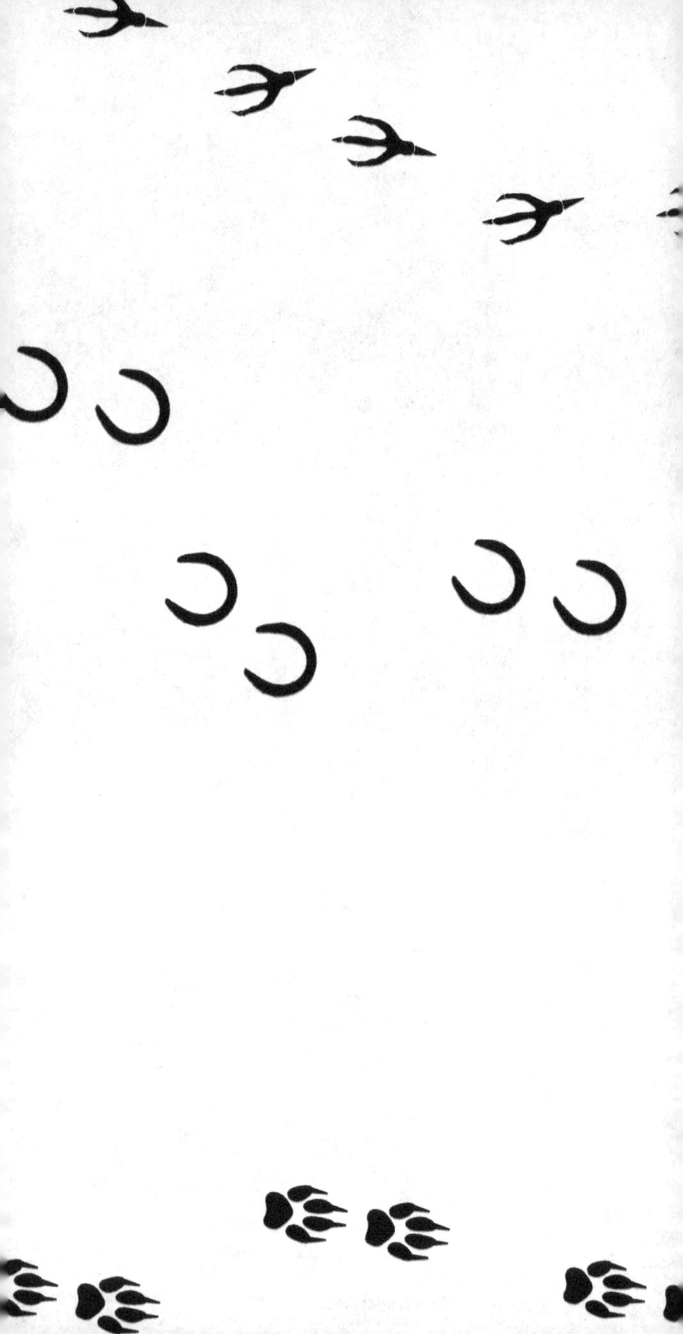

TO THE SOUL FRIENDS
THAT HAVE SHARED THEIR LIVES WITH ME,
&
THE WILD ANIMALS
THAT HAVE ENDLESSLY INSPIRED ME.

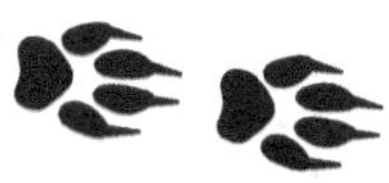

L▽VE

Nourish the earth
and all that walk it.
Allow the force
of the Universe
to guide you.

•

DIVINITY

TIPSY

Eddy's Motel
Butte Montana

I can't sleep,
the stagnant smell of mold,
smoke,
and dirty skin
keep me awake.

I self-medicate
with a bottle of Jack.

A storm hits at 4 am
waking the roaches,
you tell me you love me.

IN THE NIGHT

To me,
you are the moon.

My soul is hungry
like the wolves
I hear howl
in the Tetons.

I am the wolf,
you are the moon.

MAINE

The salt kisses me softly,
as soft and sweet
as few
of my most genuine lovers.

A flower rests
near the headstone
of a man named Junkins.

I fight the desire to pick it,
if I do,
the dew drops
will have nowhere to go.

A RAT AND A HORSE

You are a rat,
I am a horse.

You are a man,
I am a woman.

You are a sea cowboy,
I am a land cowgirl.

You are night,
I am day.

You are mythology,
I am poetry.

You are a pencil,
I am a pen.

You are rock 'n roll,
I am the blues.

You are electric,
I am acoustic.

You are the tip of the boot,
I am the sole.

You are sage,
I am piñon.

You are a wall of weapons,
I am a dagger.

You are a loud, ear-piercing laugh,
I am the cause.

You are giving,
I am the thief

of all the clothes
in your closet.

A MUSICIAN

Map of the world,
red lights,
Levi's,
your white shirt
against my thighs.

I admire the way
your eyes
pour over
the paper.

A private place,
a place you once
wrote rhythmic words.

You pause to pull in
an old emotion,
I pause with you.

I read you,
the same way
you read
the notes of a new song.

ARMSTRONG CREEK

'70s mustard vinyl,
forest green shag.

Your father sips
his homemade raspberry wine
out of a German pint glass.

Sweet pickled beets
and a joint of L.A. sunshine.
Blackjack tips 'n tricks
tapping the table to moonrise.

Bangladeshi records spin
on the turntable,
Bella the cat hisses.
Wine stains
the smiles of the table
red.

UP NORTH

This morning,
the mosquitos
and your green eyes
are wide awake.

Ripples race
across the lake.

The rain graced us
last night,
muddying our dreams.

IT BURNS

You make us bacon, eggs,
and beans over the fire.

I'm surprised you're clothed,
you're usually naked.

We sway to Karen Dalton,
grease from the cast iron
smacking our skin.

ROOMS

In this apartment,
we share our lives.

It is not mine.
It is not yours.
It is not ours.
It is a file in some rich man's cabinet
down by the bay.

I feel free in this one-bedroom apartment,
as if I have rooms upon rooms to discover.

You are all the rooms
I've never had.

ROOM 411

Dearest Marco,
you are a Wizard.

Blue eyes,
hair as stark white
as the oxygen tank
at your feet.

Your energy skips about,
taking my hand,
pulling me through unearthly realms.

Your heart is as light
as the feathers
placed perfectly
in pages of poetry
throughout your loft.

You hand me a shark tooth,
a baby alligator,
a ball of turquoise
the size of my fist,
and send me on my way.

THOUGHT

I do not read enough,
a fresh breeze interrupts my thought.
A book props open the window.

ANABELLA

Brooklyn street stories
over whiskey and Campari.

Cheating boyfriends with backbones
matching hero shrews.
The way your eyeliner carefully
picked a new color
from the rainbow
to paint your eyes each morning.

We built a fort
so we could disappear under the sheets,
so for once
you could just feel safe
from the heartless people
who took you there unwillingly.

One needle
marked my initials on your chest,
between your breasts,
heart,
and every goddamn perfect part of you.

I PRAY
you never forget how valuable you are.
I pray you never forget
the miles will never get longer
or shorter between us.

I PRAY
the only thing that will get longer is your hair.
The only thing that will get shorter is your
hair.
Hair is all you need to worry about, really.

I PRAY
whoever he is,
he is paying for you to get your hair done.

FOR A FRIEND

You cannot keep a person warm
with a sugar coat.

But you can feel whole
with holes.

LOVER FOR A NIGHT

The bar we met at was crowded,
tobacco clouds fading every so often
to catch our gaze.

You kiss an old lover
on her forehead,
as we stumble to our exit.

Your English is broken,
my Spanish in pieces.
Finding conversation
through hand gestures
and aligned eyes
on comfortable couches in Malasaña.

Fantasy unravels in liquor,
pieces of hair stray from your crown,
I misplace them occasionally
with any nerves I might have.

I close the gates of your hurt heart
with my lips.

You seem a bit lost,
but so am I.
It feels right to find each other,
for just one night.

You confess imaginary love to me.
Your words float like sail ships
to my shore.

"I love you"
over and over,
again and again.

I let you lie,
because I can tell you just miss saying it,
loudly,
to a stranger you barely know.

SOLANA BEACH

Fog zombies and cliff debris.
The view was ideal,
palm trees, coast, and rich people,
but really my interest was in her.

Her posture,
the way her mind pondered
when she lifted her cigarette.

This was just the beginning.
The beginning smelled of salt and menthol.

CALIFORNIA

The sun hits the windshield,
casting a halo of nostalgia
around my head.

In every rodeo I pass,
I see my mother
racing her horse Tammy,
a denim tuxedo and cash trophy
to pay her college dues.

I see my father,
his gaze steady across the water,
the Milky Way and a waning moon
lighting his way.
Catching and releasing
all but tomorrow's dinner.

The smell of wild rose
and California peonies
creeps into my nostrils.

My lungs fill with memories,
the woman I miss
and the man I grew to forgive.

EAST BOUND

Dear California,
I draw breath in Arizona now.
I miss your briney kiss,
and the man by the bay
shucking oysters.

When I crossed the border,
I crossed my heart and hoped to die.
A promise,
I would see you again.

DEAR COYOTE

By the time you read this,
I'll be thousands of miles away,
preparing to face anacondas, sickness,
and a past life of love and buried pain.

If I am afraid,
I know your light will search for me,
draw me out of the darkest places.

Miles between us
are only empty lots of bridges
you will build.

If I close my lids and tremble,
will you take my hand
to the orange couch
across from the wood-burning fireplace?

I know you will.

FOR YOU

I love you bitter,
I love you sweet.

I love you when the dove cries,
and when the owl speaks.

I love you in the sunshine,
and when the clouds are bleak.

I love you bitter,
I love you sweet.

WILDFLOWER

Your room is the color
of Indian paintbrush,
the wildflower
you find
along the asphalt
in Idaho.

Sweet grass burns,
I crack the window.
The smoke exits
with any spirits
no longer welcome.

S▽RR▽W

*Let water fall
from the sky above
to the corner of your eyes
and soil beneath you.*

☽

GROWTH

LUPO SOLITARIO

My mind has gone dark,
dark as the fur that stands high
on the lone wolf's back
before it turns from its pack
forever.

I AM A BIRD TOO

I hope to never tame your wild spirit.
It is what I love most
about you.

I notice your wings beginning to clip,
I understand
the way it torments you.

The thought of staying in one place,
waking up next to each other every day,
and actually enjoying it.

STANDING ROCK

My mind races like a wild horse
while the moon rotates slowly above the pines.
Thoughts travel down my back
and over my sides.

My slumber is sliced open
by the ice of the air;
as the distant hum haunts,
invasion comes clear.

The dawn
is swept off by the sun,
along with the clouds,
the dirt, and the fog.

Elders pass tobacco,
a pinch to pay a prayer,
the fire eats it up,
the flame becomes its ears.

The peace of their land,
the sacred promise it holds,
disrupted by thieves
and unforgiving ghosts.

Tribes of warriors
face the muzzles of men,
and there,
history repeats itself
again and again.

MNI WICONI
WATER IS LIFE

TALLY

She slits her wrists,
horizontal wounds.

A score to keep count,
all the men
that have come and gone.

SELJALANDSFOSS

Iceland's black sand beaches
take film from me,
the way the tide rises to take the shore.

Waterfalls stream down mountaintops,
tears of agony
cover Mother Earth's face,
plunging into
a pool
of ineffable distress.

To the bystander,
euphoria.

FLORENCE

Here I am,
in the most beautiful city in the world,
crying my eyes out
because I look like my mother.

BALSAMIC SCARS

I pour balsamic into an olive oil dish
and watch it take shapes similar to small scars.

A bottle of sangiovese hits my lips,
painting them red,
the way an artist would give his last breath
to paint this city.

Tears stack against my face,
like the row of pastel buildings
running parallel to Ponte Vecchio.

Silently searching for solace,
I head towards a garden of Roman gods,
hoping to find strength and solution in their
eyes carved from stone.

To this day, I am unsure how,
but the moss-covered men, women,
and mammals spoke
volumes to my unsettled heart.

I began to understand
the unbearable pain of loss
and the darkness that can follow.
And there,
in the Boboli Gardens of Florence,
my despair was overcome
by the Panacean power of light.

BLOOD

I took the life of a mosquito
in the bathroom.

Left unchanged.

MOHER

The Cliffs were quiet,
common gulls at eye level.

The afternoon light
contrasted the primary colors,
colors only to be captured
in great paintings or film.

Tall beds of soft, moss-like flora
covered the eroded shale and sandstone.

I watched their bodies lean
just far enough over the edge
to disturb any imagination
of the wandering passerby.

Women carelessly dozed in scurvy grass,
picking petals off Sheep's-bit
to verify the love
of the uncertain lover.

The sun eventually decided to nod off
with each of them on the cliffside,
but their eyes had now glimpsed a light
too great to ever let go...

They ran as fast as they could to the very end,
as if they would never see the sun again,
as if it would never awake
and the moon would hold its colors
captive forever.

AMERICA

I am not afraid,
I am paralyzed with fear.

To return home
to a place
where we rush moments
to make moments.

NOT MY HANDS

I am no longer a girl
but a women "nesting"
in a one-bedroom flat,
no diamond,
no child,
no lover.

My fertility clock ticks,
I attempt to smash it.
My childbearing hips remind me
I am a fool for trying.

NARNIA

This morning,
we dance in Narnia,
the magic lights
blinding our retinas.

We climb under jagged,
wired fences
and swing from vines
over rivers
made from rain.

Every so often,
we speak our fears.
Die laughing.
Then die inside.

It is there, inside,
we host a funeral,
arranging wild violets
atop our caskets.

A secret gathering of one,
amongst three.

POETRY

The cabin smells
of chopped garlic cloves
and the sea.

We bump hips
unintentionally,
stepping on toes,
propane stove.

The rain falls
onto delicate webs
the spiders have woven.

Three logs
and sheep's wool
start the perfect fire.

A little black book
of Leonard Cohen poems,
lantern light and wine
spill across the pages.

Tears fall from
just one of my eyes.
The way he speaks of change.
My muse lies on the ground
acting out loneliness.
Her blonde curls
drape over the dirt.

The smell of scallops lingers,
the cabernet is gone.
The empty liter sits
under the bench,
in the rain,
alone.

The moose skull above our cabin
makes me ponder life and death.

ALONE

I am a coward,
afraid to write
because I am in denial.

We have begun to lose each other.
The good and the bad memories
have ceased to claim their threshold.

Now,
I am just floating on a cloud
after this storm of ours.

METH

An abandoned
burnt-down whorehouse
crumbles at the edge
of an old silver mining town.

A whiskey neat at Yesterdays.
A yard of garbage.
A man with a horse's mane
as black as the tower of trash
he stands on.
A true knight
in shining aluminum.

Ten-to-five,
a strain of sativa.
The shack owner
blurts,

"stay away;"
"he's no good;"
"he's an addict."

So was she,
a true womb-kicker,
with a dusted wig
and a witch chin.

ANXIETY

Never invited.
Always shows up.
Wreaks havoc.
Leaves.

LEMON WALLEYE

My brittle black hair.
Your unmarred mane of curls.
Discarding my egg whites
along with paranoid premonitions
of a life without you.

The smell of our prized lemon grilled walleye
flooded the kitchen.
I sat in an unusual silence
as a blanket of warm, golden light
fell from ceiling fixtures
onto your spleen scar.
The one that draws a banner
across your abdomen each day.

THE CURSE OF YOU

Today I thought about you.
Yesterday I thought about you.
Seven months before that
I thought about you.
A year ago I thought about you.

The only time I did not think about you
was before I fell in love with you.

That was a long time ago.

KENTUCKY

Our camp neighbor
has been to prison once.
Inmates paid him to roll joints.

He also did meth,
a lot of it.
The last time he did meth
was twenty years back.

His gaze strays off
as his lips force his vague eulogy.
"That drug took almost,
well, everyone I knew,"
except the girl that got away.

She still haunts his dreams,
but it's a ghost he admits creating.

"She was real once,
but there is no love
if there is no trust.
In fact, that is the moment love dies."

He turns up Cash,
"Ring of Fire,"
returning to his camp
for a quick moment
to flip his $3.79 steak
from Save A Lot.

When he returns
I light a cigar,
take a pull of Black Velvet
and ask him if he ever killed a man.
I have to because I see death above him.
I need to confront him
before he kills us, too.

He fought in Vietnam,
killing many men.
I'm not sure whether
to sleep,
feeling safe or afraid.

I chose neither.

GOODBYE FOR NOW

I see you.
I see you watch sand seep through hourglasses
as you press elevator buttons
to reach the different levels of your soul.

While you are soul-searching under stage lights
and tiptoeing around carpet fog,
I will be holding
a magnifying glass to mine under fluorescents,
if fluorescents are ever the desert sun
or dust of stars.

A ONE-SIDED CONVERSATION

The moon
mirrors itself
onto the cove.

Loons converse
about the night.

I call back,
thanking them
for their company.

THE END

I remember a time
when your boxers
took up all the space
in my underwear drawer.

I remember a time
when you would stumble home
at the crack of dawn,
hands of ice over my body.

I remember a city of "Us."
Lights alluring,
distracting us both
from red flags.

My lids double as projector screens,
a matinee.
Steam hitting the kitchen window,
you're making meat.
The humidity shapes genetic curls
around your face.

The neighbors must have thought
our love was Titanic,
all the steam
on all the windows.

THE WILD
W△M△N

Breathe into the fire
with your innermost breath,
let the flames rise
to transform you.

○

REBIRTH

A REMINDER

I bleed once a month.
I cry once a month,
and more.

If I were a man,
I would not bleed.
But,
I would cry every day,
because I am not a woman.

ECDYSIS

Bare skin and tumbleweed,
the pungent Wyoming fragrance
lures her off the highway
to heal.

There,
she molts
her skin.

Emerging
with the prairie rattlesnakes
amongst her,
the heavy haze
holding her spirit prisoner
is forced out with a clear mind.

As she transforms out of fine dust and smoke,
the desert haze knows to meet the horizon.

RIVERS

Sand slips
through my bronze fingertips.
For a moment,
slip becomes sift
and sand gold.

There is not a soul
to share my riches,
just one eel and a water beetle.

MISSOULA

Today,
our emotions took a turn
with the heat.

We are both bleeding
in Missoula,
pinching pennies
for pawn shop silver,
the kind that makes up a classic
Smith & Wesson.

We head southeast
where we find ourselves
scaling the walls
of an abandoned state prison.

An eerie hour spent
with barbed wire and birds,
or maybe they were flies,
flies the size of birds.

PEWS AND PRAIRIES

We caught an early service
at a former store, bar, now church.
Wranglers and their wives
unhurriedly filled the pews.
We hung up casual conversation
with Christians
while cowboys hung their stetsons
on curtain rods.

I watched my muse's mind drift
to places we would soon visit.
Fortunate enough to steal
her angst that morning
along with the occasional prayer.

Her head rested on my inner arm
as we prayed for rain.
Rain to heal the land
and cleanse the sins
of others.

THE ROAD

Traveling America by car,
with just a map of Indiana.

IOWA

Pastel dots float across the median.
The sun glows like a sphere
of the brightest fire I've never seen.

I swallow an Adderall at 4:56 am,
see double,
what I thought was a UFO
was really a windmill.

DNA

Southern Colorado is weird,
full of graham crackers,
grandmothers on crack.

UFO gazing signs
point to an observation deck
lined with hospital chairs
ripped from the local
psych ward.

An old German Shepherd
guards the entrance of the vortex.

The Alien Vortex,
a place where your compass spins
like tea cups at Disney
and unknown energy quiets the air.

You were supposed to leave something,
so we pissed in a plastic bottle
and placed it on the feminist quadrant
of the Vortex.

Hands covered in piss,
minds covered in disbelief,
a few more dirt roads
and a couple hundred gators later,
we were in search of the Land of Enchantment.

WHITE SANDS

Racing to the southern border,
2,000 miles and some change
just to sit on a pile of gypsum crystals.

We shed a trail of clothes
on nature's bare bosom.

Whoever said diamonds
are a girl's best friend
must have never seen the crystals
of White Sands.

KUM & GO

Shell,
BP,
On Star,
Exxon,
Mobil,
Sinclair,
Texaco,
Pilot,
Loves,
Kum & Go ...

I've pissed in about every one of 'em,
stocked up,
emptied out,
thrown down Washingtons, Lincolns,
but mostly Andrew Jacksons.
A true piece of shit he was.

POCATELLO

The light is different in Idaho.
It looks as if Iceland had a child,
and that child strayed from its Nordic ways
due to curious angst and impulse,
eventually rediscovering its roots
while making love atop obsidian mountains,
falling nothing short of brave alongside
rattlesnake thickets.

The sun encompassed her body in the car,
almost as perfect
as the 60-watt that illuminated her skin
in the Thunderbird Motel room.

I often wonder
why the lingering smell of Newport Kings
and dusted PTAC wall heaters
are so comforting,
when far from home.

OR AM I

I ain't tough as nails,
I ain't no big-fanged snake.

Just the light in the night sky,
the gentle voice when you wake.

CRATERS OF THE MOON

Sweat dripped from the rim of my sun hat
to the crease of my lips.
I was hungry as hell,
I didn't mind the taste of salt between my teeth.

I couldn't tell you
the science behind the vast land,
but after dancing and dying
for film on former beds of lava,
I am a strong believer of the Serpent Legend
of the Shoshone-Bannock tribes who inhabited
Earth's Personal Moon.

Patches of buckwheat decorated
the black ash and bed of rock,
doubling as headstones for the life beneath,
before it fell victim to the Serpent's rage.

COTTON MAGIC

I waited for the sun to rise
a bit higher before waking her,
matching her breath to mine
and the rustle of the wind
against the Ponderosa pine.

There is a song one should appreciate more,
the song of morning,
before the world wakes up.

The smoke from last night's fire
mixed with yesterday's smoked salmon
swept across the sky and into my nose.

I remember looking up
for what seemed like hours
at the crowds of cotton passing by.
Time froze in light prisms,
freeing us of mind prisons.

LAND OF GEMS

Oh, Spirit Mother of Ketchum, Idaho.
Your long white hair
whirls with the dandelions at dawn.

Your energy pulls us inward.
The black ink from your pen
bleeds onto the hand-drawn map
guiding us north and quickly west.

"A dirt road will lead you to a cemetery
hidden in the valley.
There will be a mountain of clay
covered by an afternoon shadow.
Climb till you are tired
and you will find the treasures of the earth."

The sun forces sweat
from the brim of our hats
to the bones of our collars.

Gems stick to our skin.
My muse stuffs her socks with crystals
while I stand naked,
observing her,
with nothing but a quartz necklace
to cover my chest.

We decide they are not ours to keep.
We return them to the Salmon River.

FAR AWAY

The moon
doubles in size
beyond the glass top
that is the water.

My mind a river,
flowing over the stones
that push me onward.

The clay
at the body's edge
reminds me
of the red atop
the pecker's head,
back home where I began.

MUSHROOMS

Mushrooms are not soley delicate decorations
to wounded trunks and dusky forkmoss.
They are tiny tribes of the forest floor,
healing, feeding, and taking the lives
of whoever decides to collect them.

Rivers and streams rush over
the feet of weeping cedar,
my mouth waters.

THE NATURE POEM

Laurel petals fall gracefully against the light,
each stem performing a waltz with the still air.

We travel like salmon
swimming against the current,
becoming gods
as we vanish in and out of branches.

I hand a white and black caterpillar
over to a leaf
before slipping into a pile of moss.
A true California King
in the pines of Pennsylvania.

DEER ISLE

Candle lit,
slicing Roma tomatoes,
the same way
the cicadas
slice the air.

A few wooden stumps
poke through
a pile of ferns
to join us.

BLACK MOUNTAIN

A spoonful of honey,
Mexican peanuts,
lamb,
cheese,
hyena fits,
nude creek dips,
and disposable dreams.

IVANHOE MANOR

My flat is the parlor
of a bloodless blue Mansion
built by bare hands
in the late 1800s.

The light omits
prisms of poetry onto my skin,
across, beneath, and between
my most delicate parts.

At Golden Hour,
shadows whisper
tender verse to me,

the way I imagine
Cohen whispers to Marianne.

I wonder if I have ever been a muse?
The way I feel a muse
to the star in my parlor.

LOUISIANA

Crawfish spiked
with watermelon sugar
in the bayou.

Marshmallow trails
lead to tiny dinosaurs
and their not-so-tiny mothers.

T-Rex trees line the river,
wind follows with a humid kiss.

Kingsnakes,
a pistol,
and a bed of shells
at your feet.

DOORWAYS

Cracked skin,
cracked scars,
portals to their ponder.

Conversations, affirmation and criticism
bounce about the air.

Vulnerable notions
vanish like rabbits in top hats.
My darling witches,
magicians to their own show.

WOLF MOON

The first full moon of winter,
silent, vibrating,
illuminating the palms of the L.A. foothills.

Invisible ropes bind us to the fire
and a deck of tarot.

Our feet join together,
three orbs enter our triangle,
possessing us with the forces of night.

Ecdysis,
the molting of skin,
our breasts bounce,
our phoenix nests
perch about our legs.

JOSHUA TREE

The cacti are tall,
handsome men,
begging for my attention.

I want to dance
all night with them
on the sage shag of the West.

The mountains encourage us,
shedding layers of light
across the land.

SISTER

Heading south from Taos,
the sun summoned us from the asphalt
and lackluster yellow lines
to the Garden of the Gods.

The aluminum cans
hanging from the fence posts
spoke volumes against its rays,
forcing us forward with nothing
but a glimpse of a moment in time.

We had not a single notion
of what our future would hold,
but soon we would have stories to share
through diner doors, motels,
and ramshackle saloons;
over roads of asphalt, dirt, and soot,
we had formed a bond as strong as clay.

CISCO

*"A barbershop for the living
A playground for the dead."*

It was a hot, dry morning.
The sun was no kisser either,
it was no gentle beam of light.

Scraping our skin.
Replacing our flesh
with western leather.

In the afternoon,
I watched her take my lover's identity
with a rusted pair of clippers.
Minutes later,
I watched him take hers.
Willfully losing themselves
in RV mirrors together.

I do not know much about this woman,
I just know this is her town.

I believe
not all sacred moments that come to men
are meant to be spoken,
but are to be kept atop the rocks
alongside the river bend,
or with the cougars
in the shadow of the unknown.

By the end of Cisco,
I would have lived and breathed
my dear Eileen.

*"With every shooting star
I wished a wish I'll never say.
With every shooting star she'd gasp,
and then we'd lay."*

RENO

Skyscraper lights,
escalators,
baby boomers on coke,
testosterone on gin.

Cheap cigars,
a hit of acid,
slots,
diamonds on 7s,
shrieks of excitement
when we win big.

Roulette,
free champagne,
lucky number,
red sixteen.

Another cigar,
lost it all,
Johnny Cash
sings us to sleep...

*"I shot a man in Reno
just to watch him die"*

REBIRTH

I walk along the shore,
wishing I was the mermaid
formed by children's hands.

The weight of the universe
could cover my breasts,
the way the shells
cluster about her chest.

With the crash of each wave,
I could toss all my woes to the tips,
knowing the burden
would not sit with the water,
but be carried out to sea.

LAGOA DAS FURNAS

The Queens soaked their pale bodies
in hot sulfur springs
at the base of three active volcanoes.

The archaic village of Furnas
possessed a history of Algerian pirate attacks,
notorious for stealing rams
before returning to the Barbary Coast
they came from.

Identifying as a ram myself,
I felt oddly at peace surrounded by fire
and the idea of past mutiny.

SAO MIGUEL

A dirt road
led by sixth sense
to the Atlantic.

Imperfect notes
from a ukulele
fade fast
down a labyrinth staircase
to the mouth of the sea.

The waves flood the shore
with five barrels of emotions,
hidden in the holsters
at our hips.

Gray sea tears,
a can of sardines,
a brick of brie,
and a shoe
to open a corner store bottle of red
we threw our coins together for.

We fell into conversation
the same way the rocks fell
from the hepatic-covered cliffs above us
to the seats beneath us,

sharing in growth
with the moss
and crack creatures
at our feet.

EMPTY DISCO

I wipe the crust from my eyes
and croissant flakes from my night dress.
The Mediterranean rocks me awake
on a ship to Italy.

The sun rises from the east,
my eyes scan the waves
for pilot whales
as Billie Holiday's voice travels across the bow.

Later,
drunk off cheap wine,
we slip into our best gowns
to discover sick thrills in middle-aged men.

Their addictions were many,
but that night
it was the way we danced.

I CALL HER MOTHER

I call her "Mother,"
with mindful hesitation to shorten her name,
like her story,
long and wild.
Wildly chosen by others.

Her fire has been many flames
and at times,
sulfur and snuff in the night,
but she burns.

Her wounded wings continue to heal
by the unearthed power
of the great numens of each day.

So,
I call her "Mother."

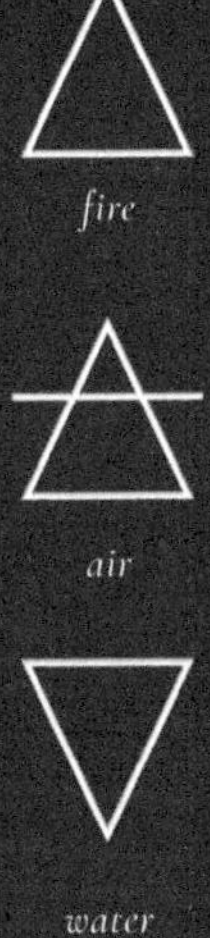

fire

air

water

earth